Hidden Seeds

HOPE FOR PARENTS

Text by Peter Wrigley
Photographs by Susannah Wrigley

Almond Tree Publishing Company

First Published in 2007 by Almond Tree Publishing Company Limited
East Poynings, Uffculme, Cullompton, Devon EX15 3AQ

Design and typography © 2007 Almond Tree Publishing
Text © 2007 Peter Wrigley
Photographs © 2007 Susannah Wrigley

All rights reserved. No part of this publication may be reproduced, stored in a retrieval system, or transmitted in any form or by any means, electronic, mechanical, photocopying, recording or otherwise, without the prior permission of the copyright owners.

ISBN 978-0-9556299-0-7

Unless otherwise indicated all scripture quotations are from the New International Version of the Holy Bible.

Scripture quotations taken from the Holy Bible, New International Version,
copyright © 1973, 1978, 1984 by International Bible Society.
Used by permission of Hodder & Stoughton Publishers, a member of the Hodder Headline Group. All rights reserved.

Scripture taken from the New King James Version, copyright © 1982 by Thomas Nelson, Inc. Used by permission. All rights reserved.

The Living Bible copyright © 1971 Tyndale House Publishers, Inc., Wheaton, Illinois 60189, All rights reserved.

Extracts from the Authorised Version of the Bible (The King James Bible), the rights in which are vested in the Crown, are reproduced by permission of the Crown's Patentee, Cambridge University Press.

Printed and bound in England by Brightsea Press Limited, Exeter EX5 2UL

*Dedicated
to the One who loves us,
Jesus Christ,
our Lord and King.*

INTRODUCTION

Our loving Father God speaks to us in many different ways and he knows the most effective way to communicate with each one of us. In addition to his written word in The Bible, he sometimes chooses to speak to our spirit through the ordinary things around us, especially through his creation.

For some people this may be difficult to accept, but it is Biblical. In the Book of Jeremiah, he says:

The word of the Lord came to me:

"What do you see Jeremiah?"

"I see the branch of an almond tree," I replied.

The Lord said to me,

"You have seen correctly, for I am watching to see that my word is fulfilled. Jeremiah 1:11-12

It seems that the Hebrew words for 'almond tree' and 'watching' sound similar to each other. Isn't it great that God himself plays with words to get his meaning across to us?

Some of us respond more to visual imagery than we do to the written word. God told Abraham to look up and count the stars in the sky so that he would understand the multitude of his offspring. Jesus told parables about life using pictures of seeds and weeds, wolves and snakes, lambs and doves, sparrows and pearls, in order to teach the people around him.

The Holy Spirit still does the same for us. For me, it is usually the beautiful things of God's creation such as flowers and birds. We are all unique and God's way of communicating with us is equally unique.

The following pages describe an occasion when I was sitting alone in our garden. It was a time when we were facing serious challenges as a family. We still are! The air was very clear, the sky bright blue and the sun warm on my back, even though it was late January. What God then showed me gave me great hope for the future and encouraged me to trust him when there seemed to be no evidence to show how things could change.

As you read the words and look at the pictures, may the God of hope encourage you too.

Hidden Seeds

To my left, *golden* crocuses were clustered in the grass where they were planted some years ago. In the blazing sun, some were bigger and more extravagantly *gold* than they had ever been before, and they had opened out their petals wide in response to the warmth.

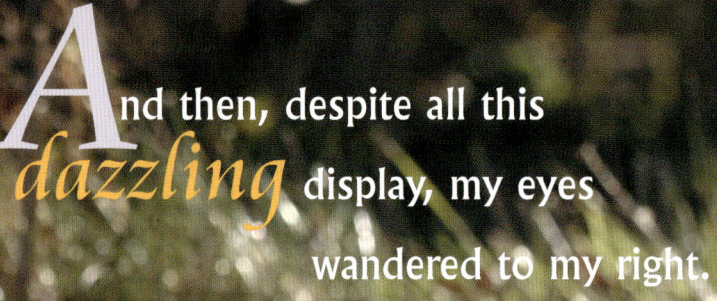

And then, despite all this *dazzling* display, my eyes wandered to my right.

There, very delicate and very beautiful, were new crocus flowers that had not been there before. When I counted them, there were fifty-three.

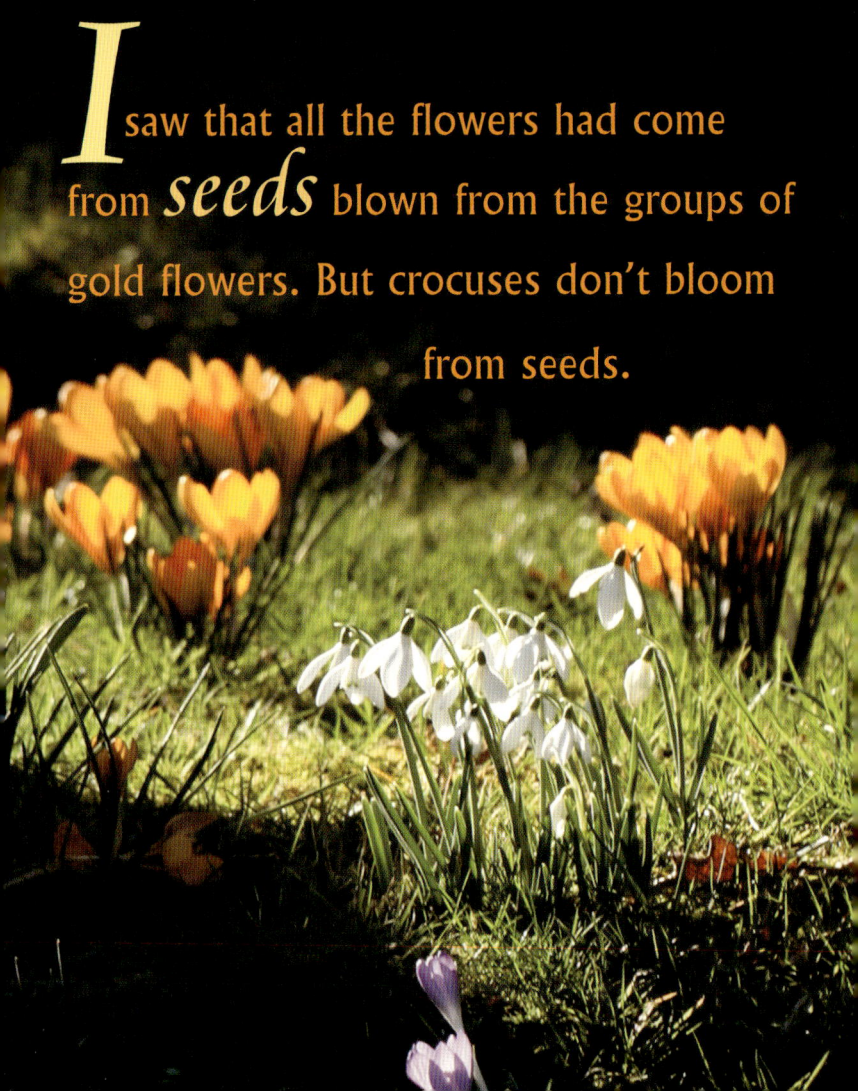

I saw that all the flowers had come from *seeds* blown from the groups of gold flowers. But crocuses don't bloom from seeds.

Perhaps as long as five years ago, the seeds had settled unseen among the blades of grass, on fertile ground. Then they had germinated and grown until the secret corms were ripe for *flowering*.

It had taken time.

As I looked, God showed me that this is like areas of our lives. He told me that we had sown spiritual seeds in the past that we have not yet seen produce a harvest. We were probably even unaware of some of the seeds. Totally unbeknown to us, the seeds were blown *where the Spirit chose* and were being watered by *God himself.*

*L*ike the new crocuses, some of the seeds have produced very *delicate, fragile-looking* plants that need nurturing and protecting; others are the bold, strong colours of the parent plants.

*S*ome are standing on their own ...

Others are clustered in groups like families. But they all have their own *pollen* and the ability to grow.

I realised that the seeds which had been sown into our children's lives, either by us or by others, which have not yet been seen to bear fruit, *will* do so.

These things I plan won't happen right away. Slowly, steadily, surely, the time approaches when the vision will be fulfilled. If it seems slow, do not despair, for these things will surely come to pass. Just be patient! They will not be overdue a single day!

HABAKKUK 2:3 (TLB)

The seed of the righteous shall be delivered.

PROVERBS 11:21 (KJV)

All your children shall be taught by the Lord and great shall be the peace of your children.

ISAIAH 54:13 (NKJV)

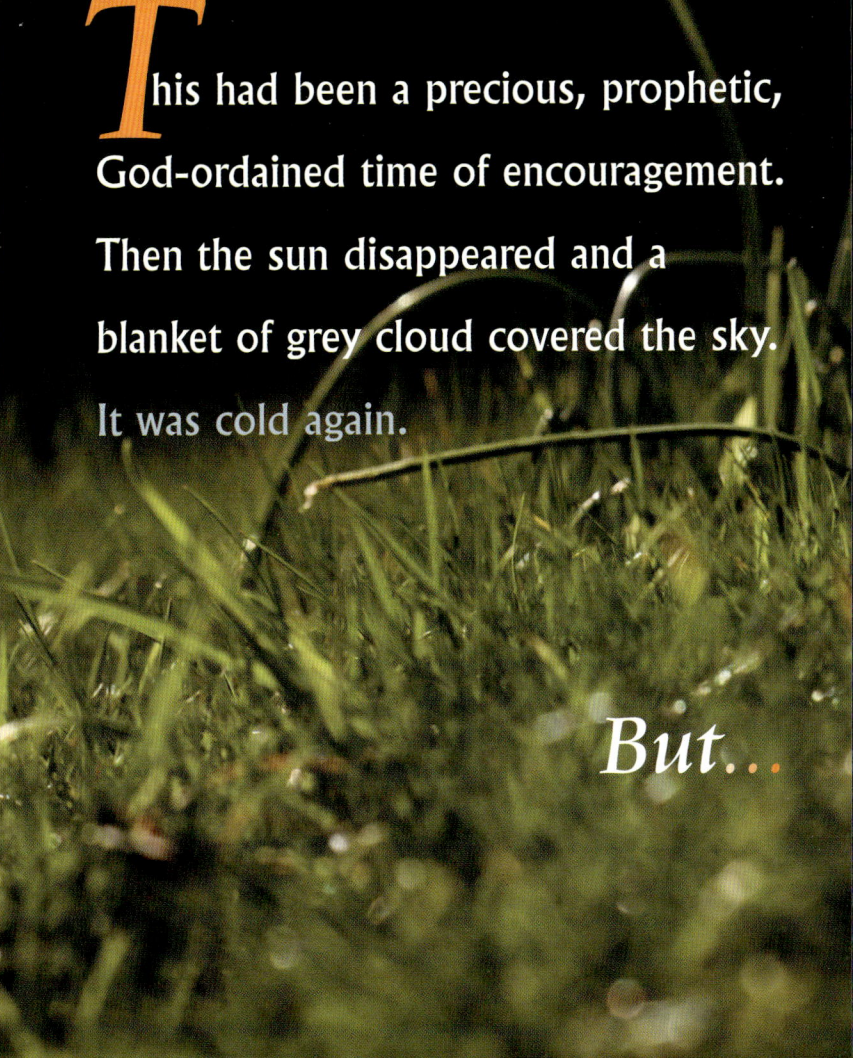

This had been a precious, prophetic, God-ordained time of encouragement. Then the sun disappeared and a blanket of grey cloud covered the sky. It was cold again.

But...

... the golden crocuses to my left blazed like the *glory* of the LORD.

And the purple crocuses to my right stood as reminders of the promises of God and of his power *to fulfil them.*

FURTHER SCRIPTURES ABOUT OUR CHILDREN

"Believe in the Lord Jesus, and you will be saved -- you and your household."   Acts 16:31

"I will pour out my Spirit and my blessings on your children."   Isaiah 44:3b (TLB)

But this is what the Lord says:
   "... I will contend with those who contend with you, and your children I will save."   Isaiah 49:25

I was young and now I am old, yet I have never seen the righteous forsaken or their children begging bread. They are always generous and lend freely: their children will be blessed.   Psalm 37:25-26

This is what the Lord says:

"A voice is heard in Ramah, mourning and weeping, Rachel weeping for her children and refusing to be comforted, because her children are no more."

This is what the Lord says:

"Restrain your voice from weeping and your eyes from tears, for your work will be rewarded," declares the Lord. "Your children will return to their own land."

JEREMIAH 31:15-17

[Jesus said:]

"In the same way your Father in heaven is not willing that any of these little ones should be lost."

MATTHEW 18:14

PRAYING THE PROMISES OF GOD

There is power in taking God's word and speaking it out loud as an agreement with him. There are good Biblical reasons for doing this:

When we speak God's promises out loud our own ears hear the words and our faith is increased: "Faith comes from hearing the message, and the message is heard through the word of Christ." Romans 10:17.

When we thank God for his promise before we see results (and after!) God is pleased with our response and he is able to work in our situation: "Now faith is being sure of what we hope for and certain of what we do not see. Without faith it is impossible to please God." Hebrews 11:1 & 6.

When we speak out the truth, we take authority over the lies of the Devil. This is precisely what Jesus did when

Satan tested him in the desert. By doing this we bring ourselves into agreement with God and his word, instead of being worried, oppressed, despairing or fearful of the circumstances. It can be a battle and we have to be prepared to work at it and leave the timing to God. Not everything is a quick fix.

If you have not prayed for your children like this before, you might pray along the following lines, but it is best to find your own way of talking to our Father God:

"Father, you say that all my children shall be taught by you and great will be their peace. Whatever the situation is at present, I thank you that my children will be taught by you and I thank you for their great peace. It is written that the children of the righteous shall be blessed by the Lord, so I bind up all the lies and taunts of Satan now with this word of truth. And Father, I thank you for my children as they are now. Amen".

Peter and Susannah Wrigley are father and daughter and live in Devon. This is their first book together. They would like to thank Andy for his technical expertise; Cynthia for her faith and encouragement; and special thanks to Phil and Sally whose practical support and consistent belief in us has been amazing. Thanks also to everyone who has kept on praying for us.

~*~

Further copies of this book are available from:
Almond Tree Publishing Company Limited
East Poynings, Uffculme, Cullompton
Devon EX15 3AQ
email: info@almondtreepublishing.co.uk
telephone 01884 840005

For more information about Almond Tree Publishing
and about other titles please go to:
www.almondtreepublishing.co.uk